COLORINGLIFESTYLES:
Grayscale Beauties

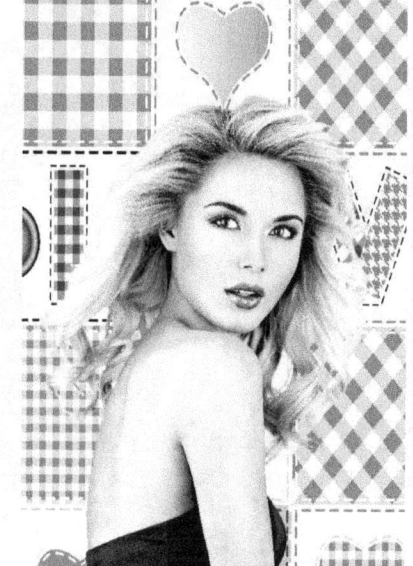

ColoringLifestyles.com
copyright@2017

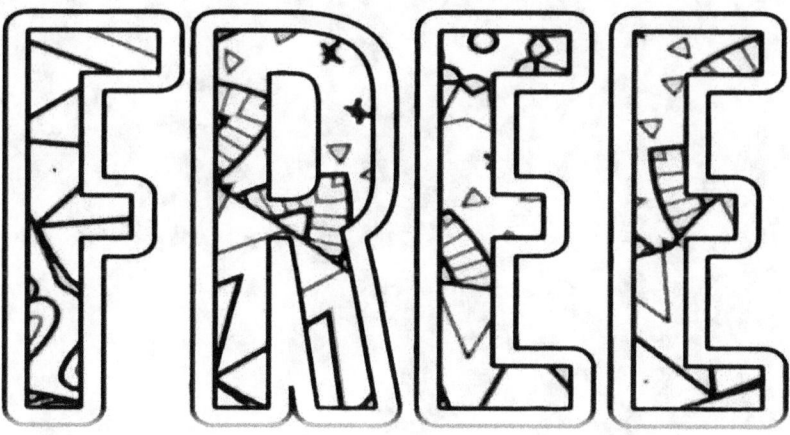

Are you anxious for your book to arrive in the mailbox? No worries! There is immediate gratification for your worried little self---so calm down! Visit ColoringLifestyles.com for information on how you can get 4 gorgeous, printable coloring sheets FREE from this very book! Start coloring today and before you know it, your coloring book will have arrived in the mail! Happy coloring and CONGRATULATIONS!

Dedicated to Donald
the love of of my life

Thank you for believing in me!

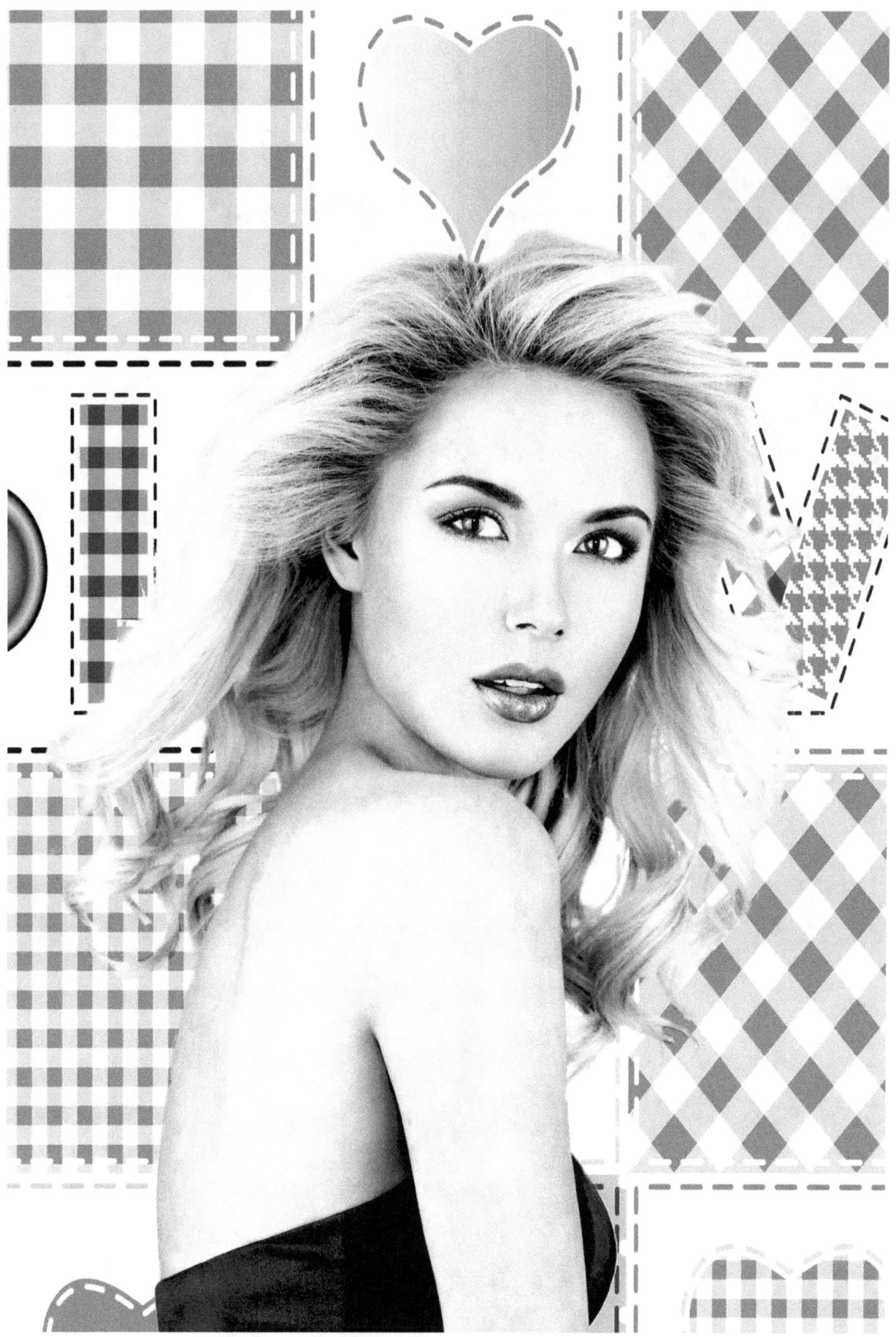

2

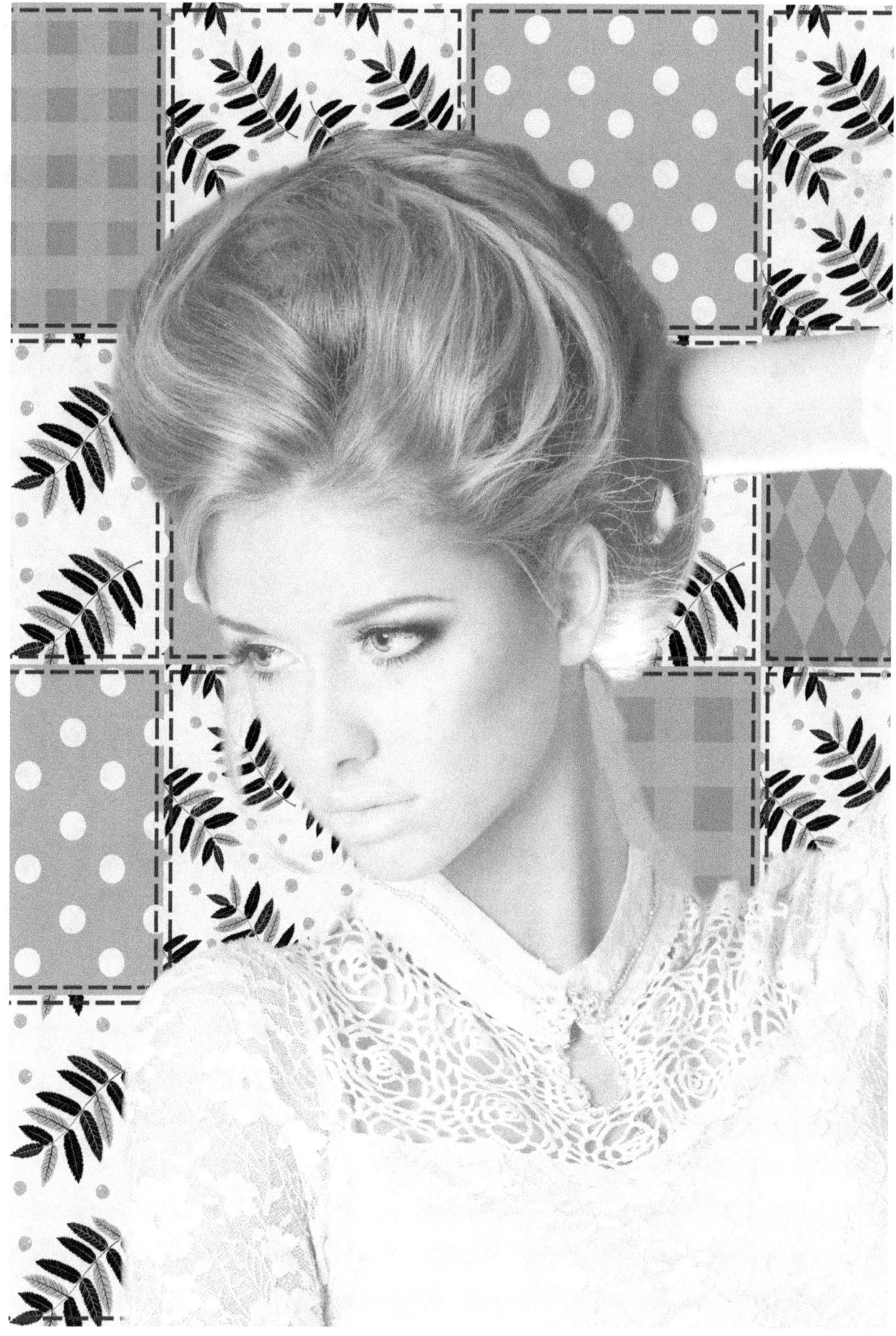

4

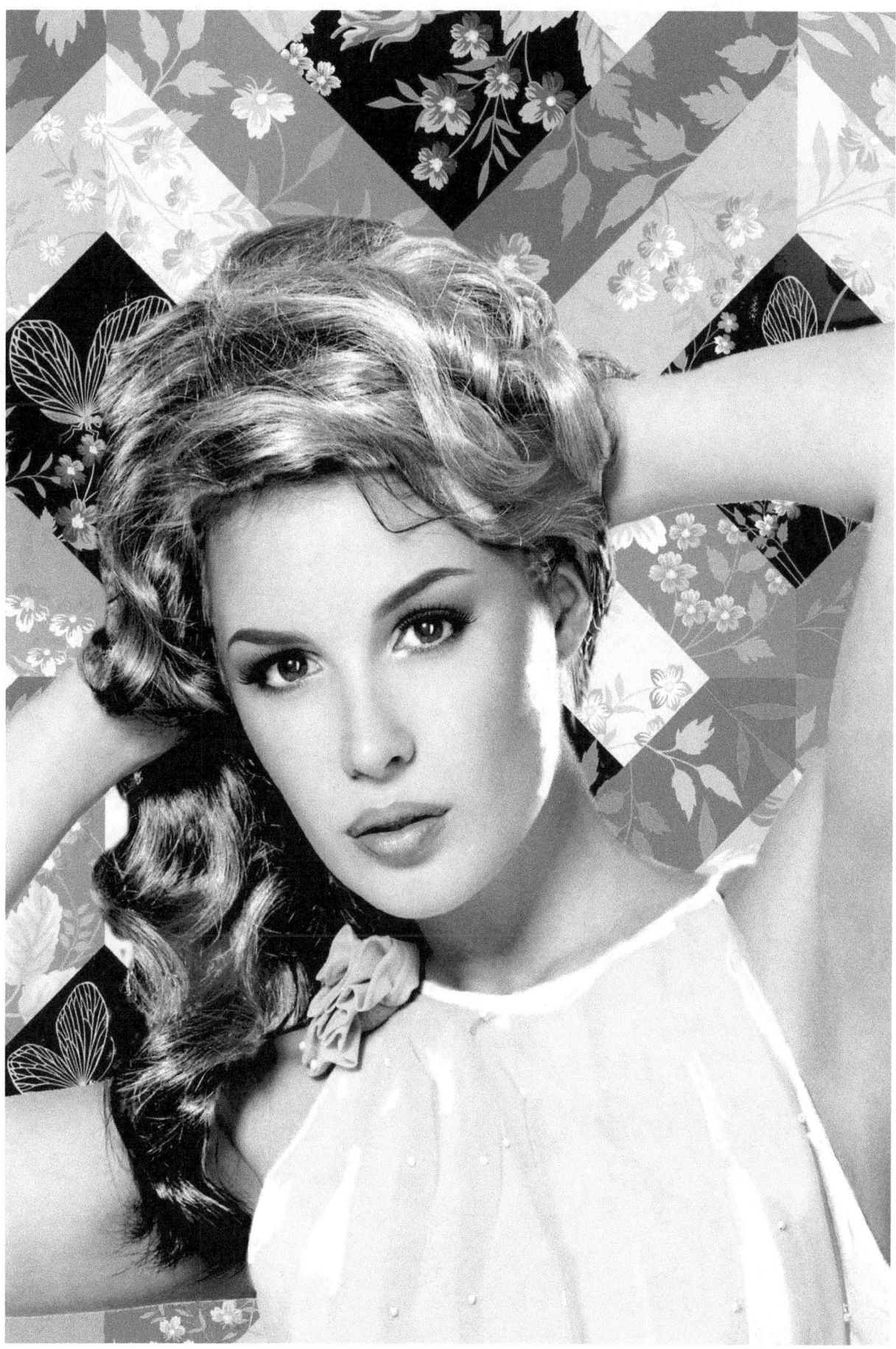

6

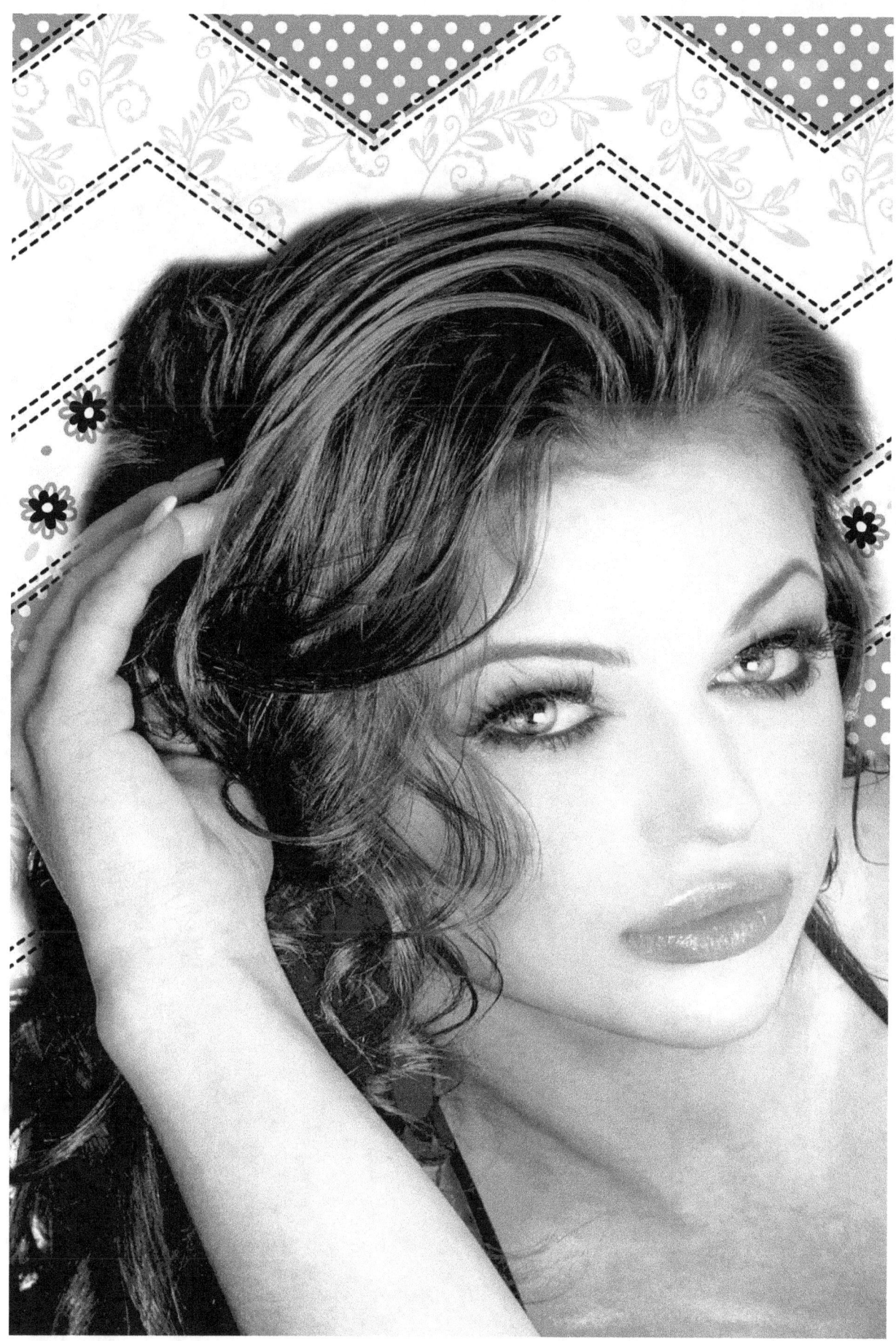

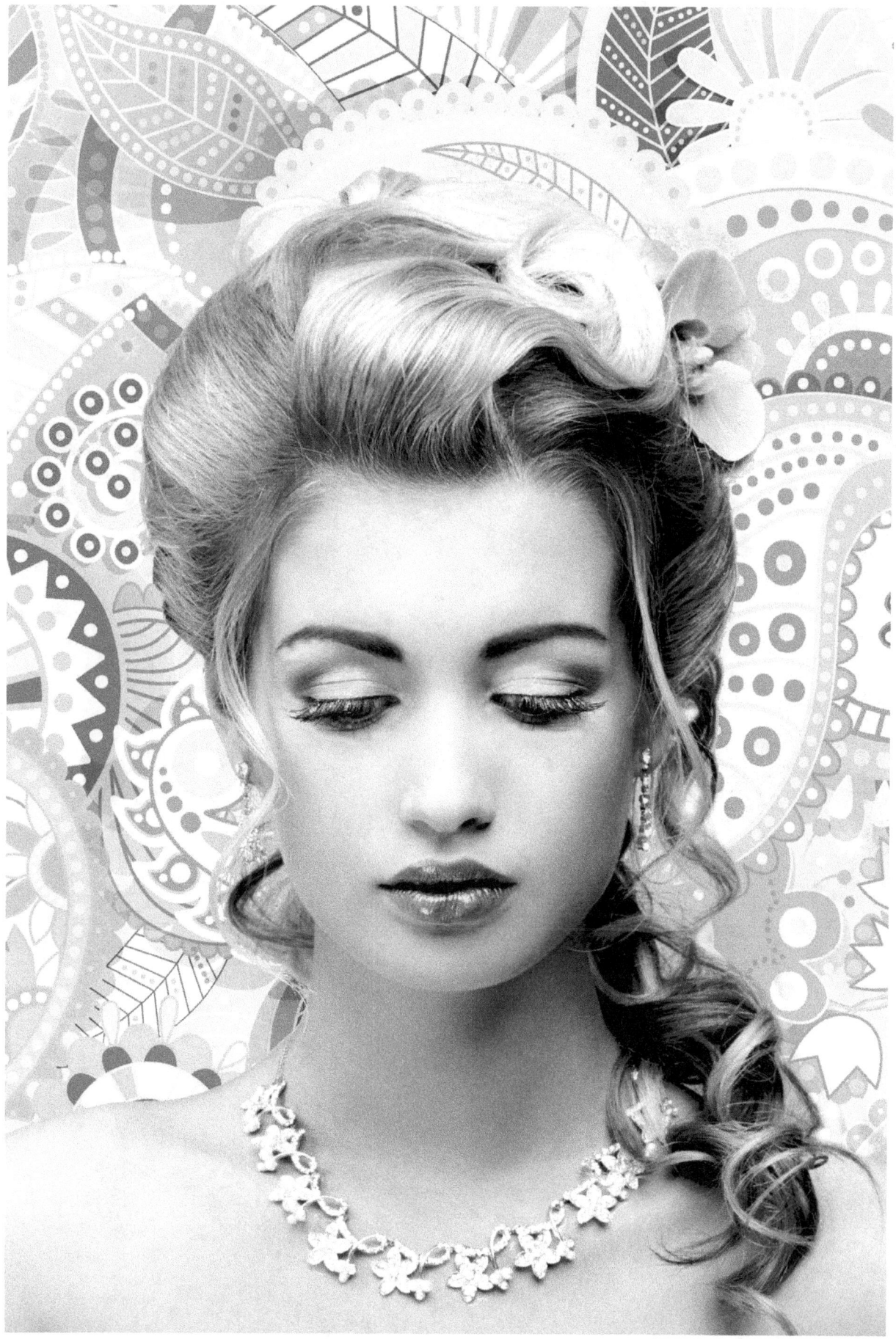

10

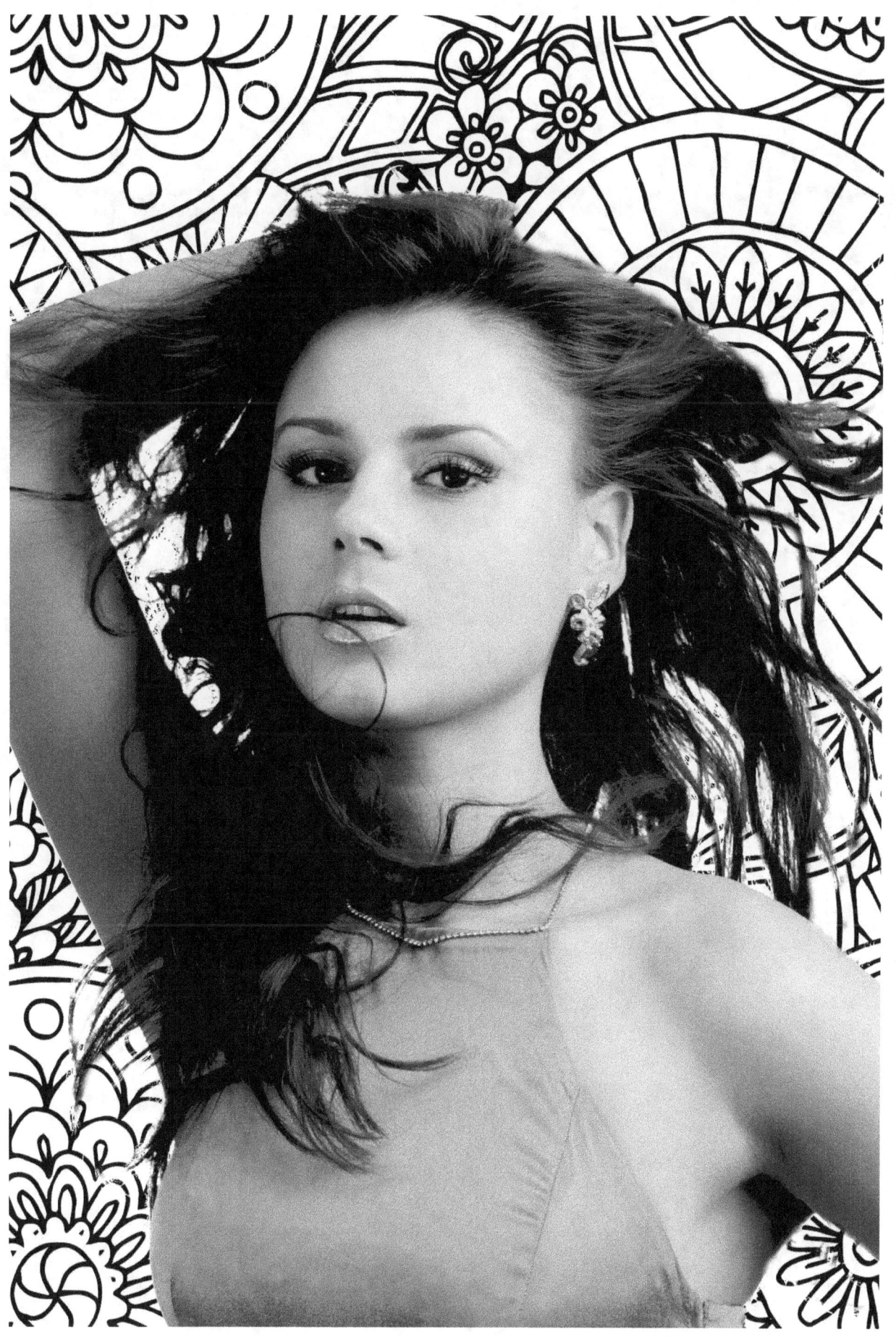

12

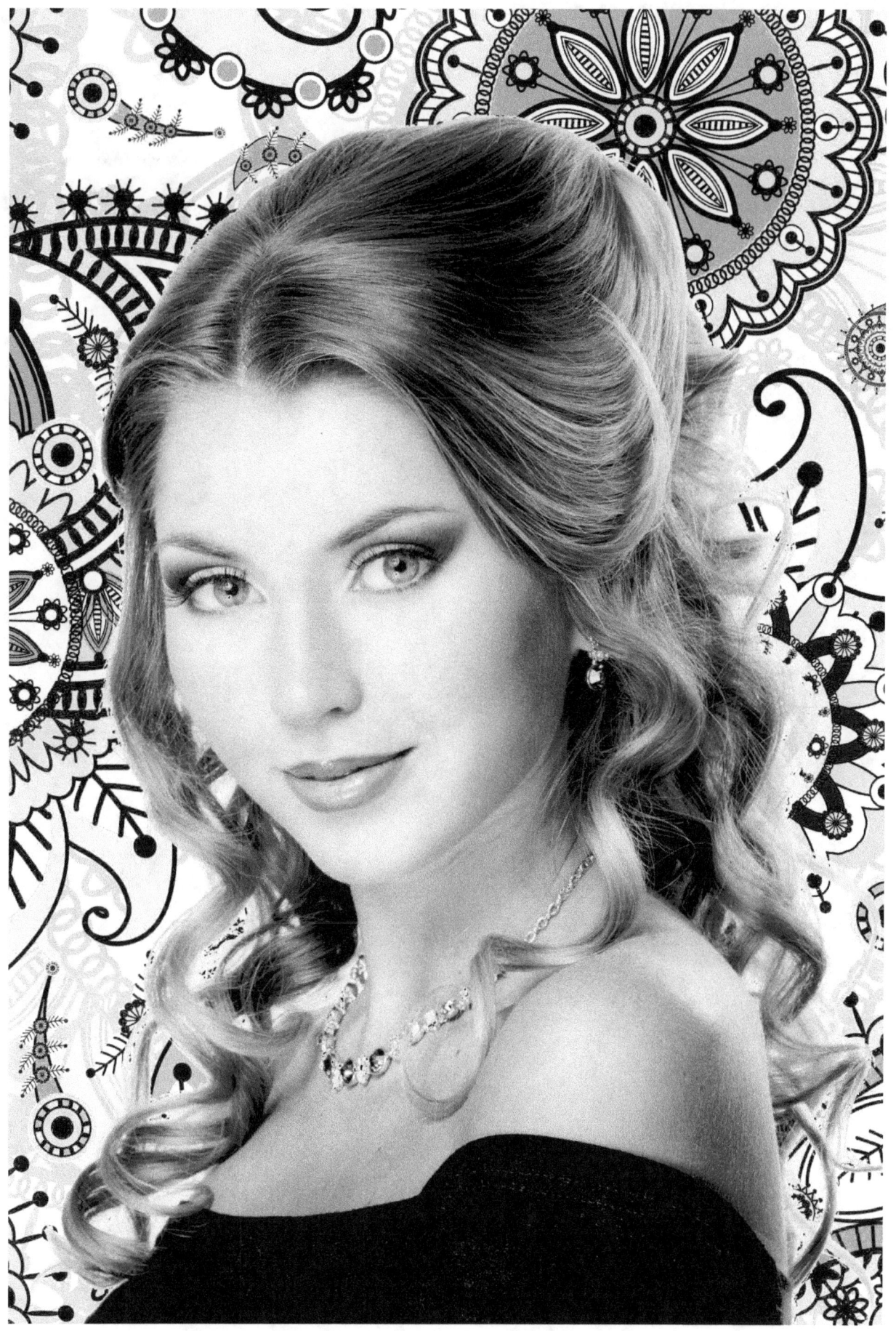

14

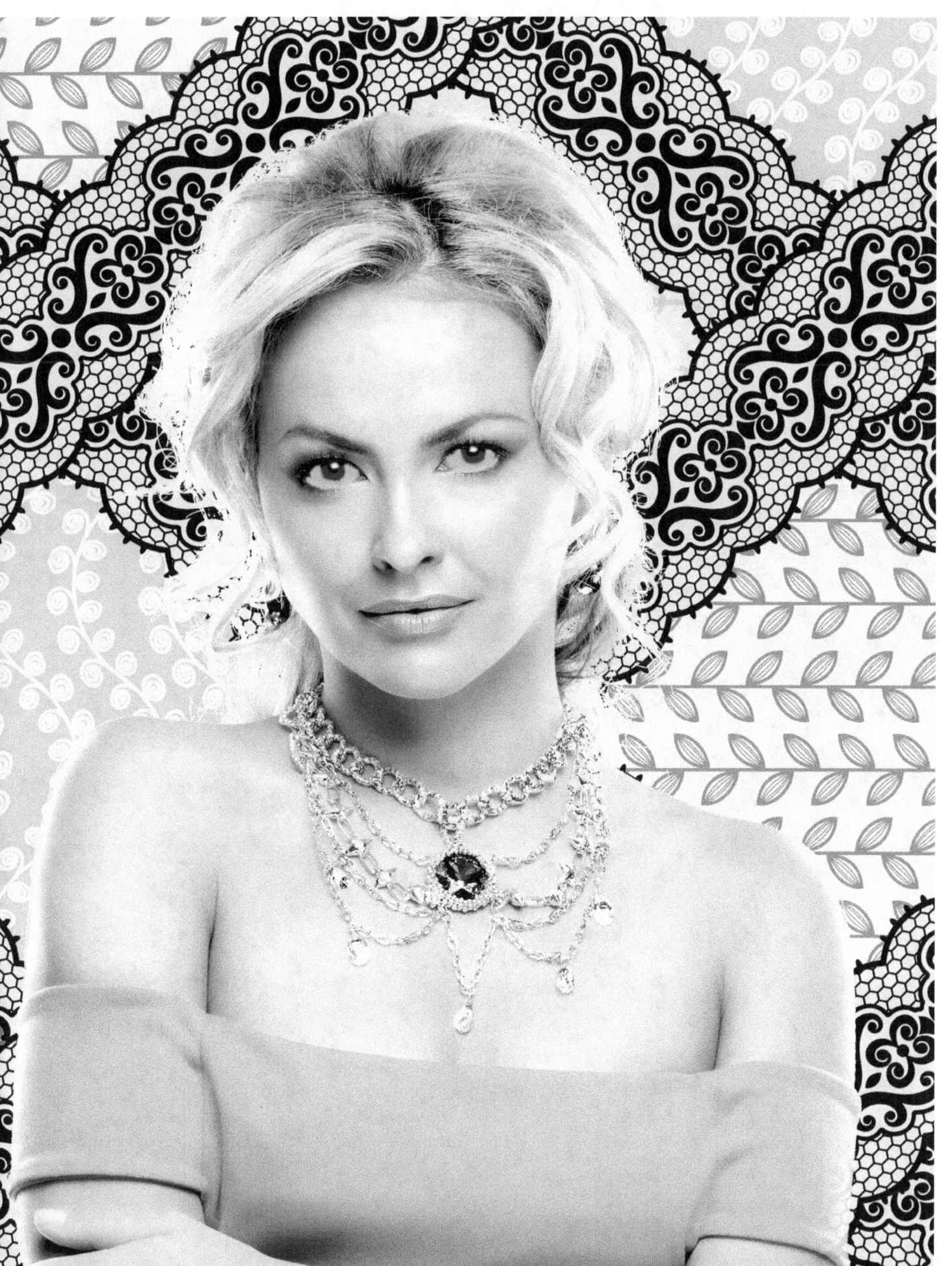

16

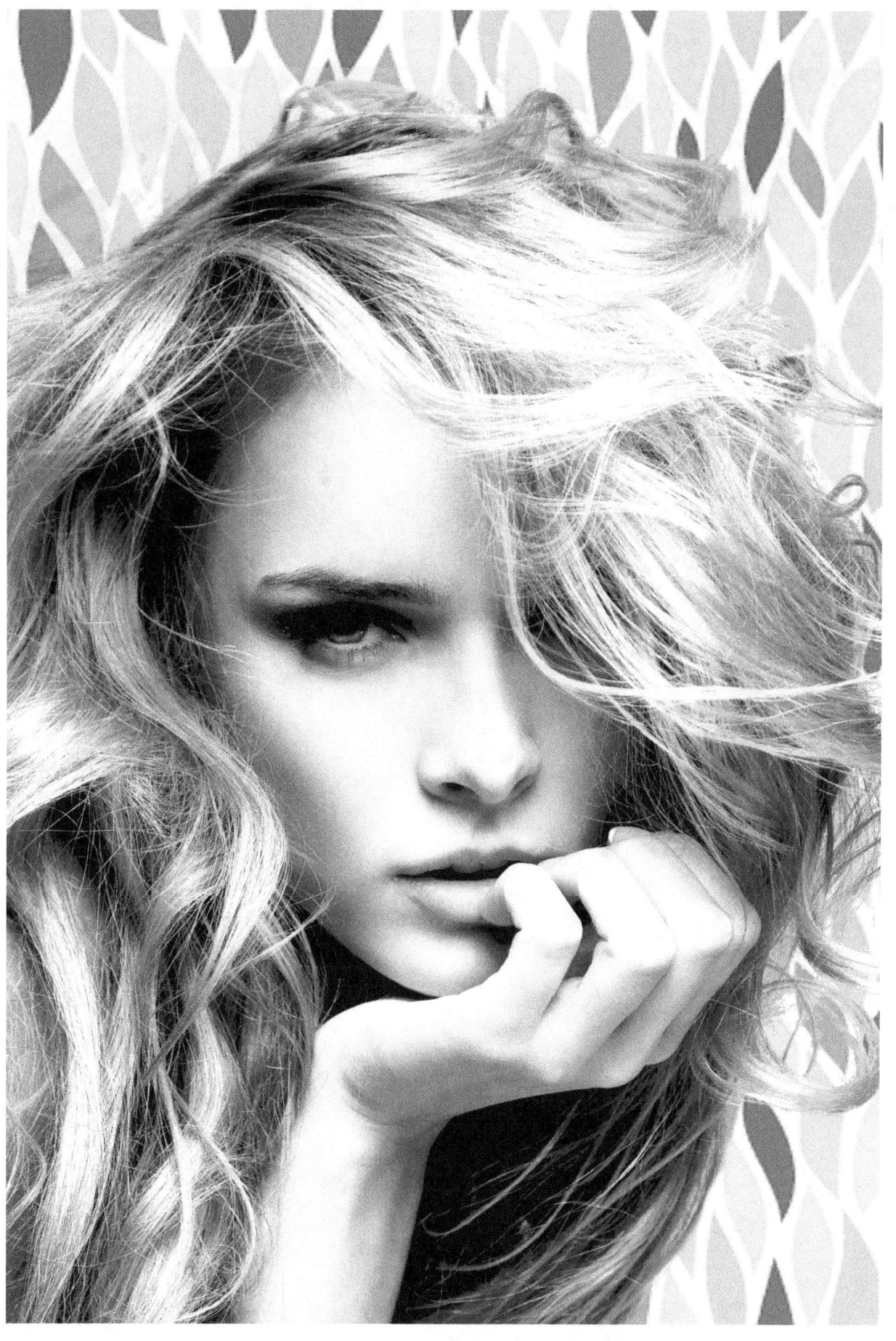

18

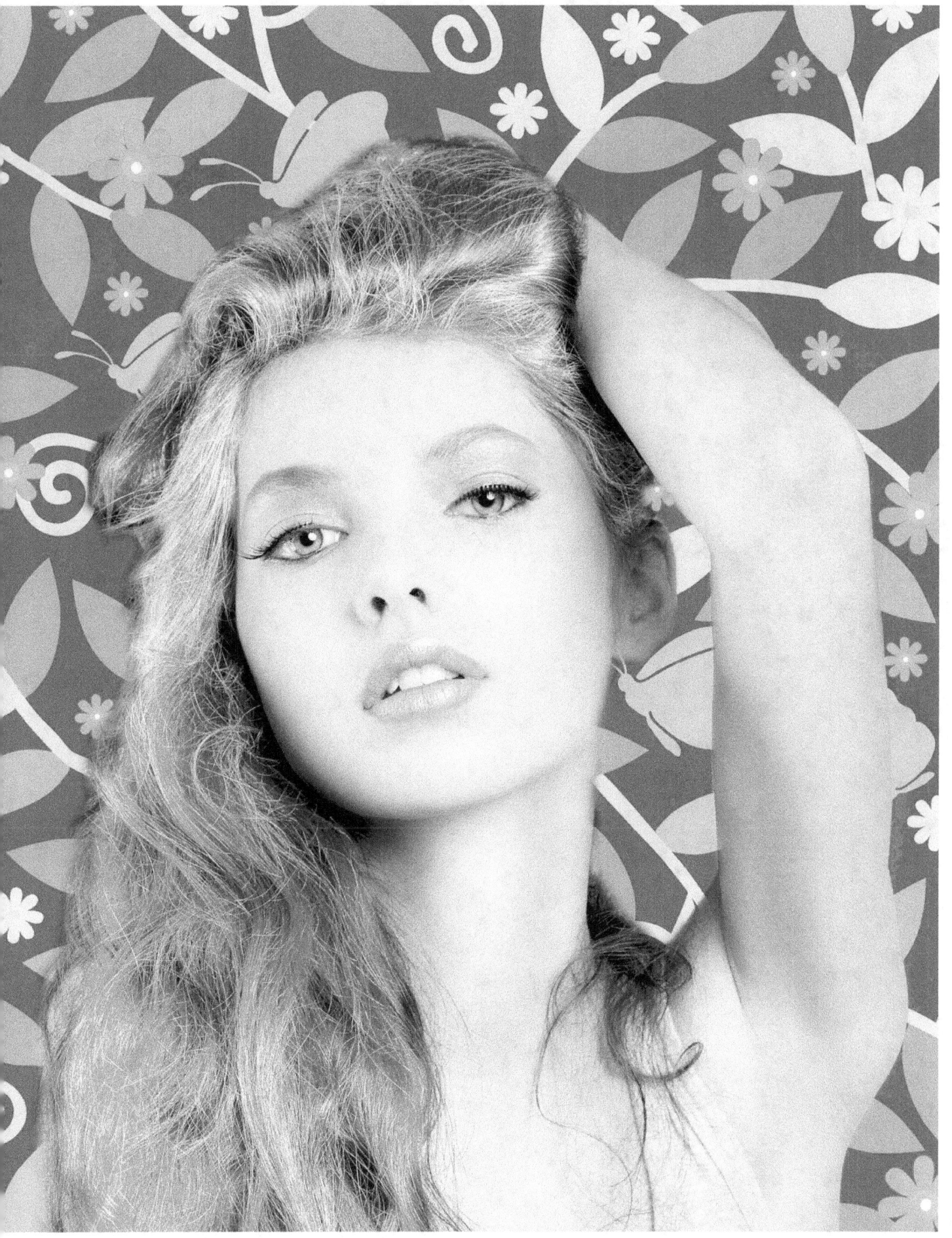

20

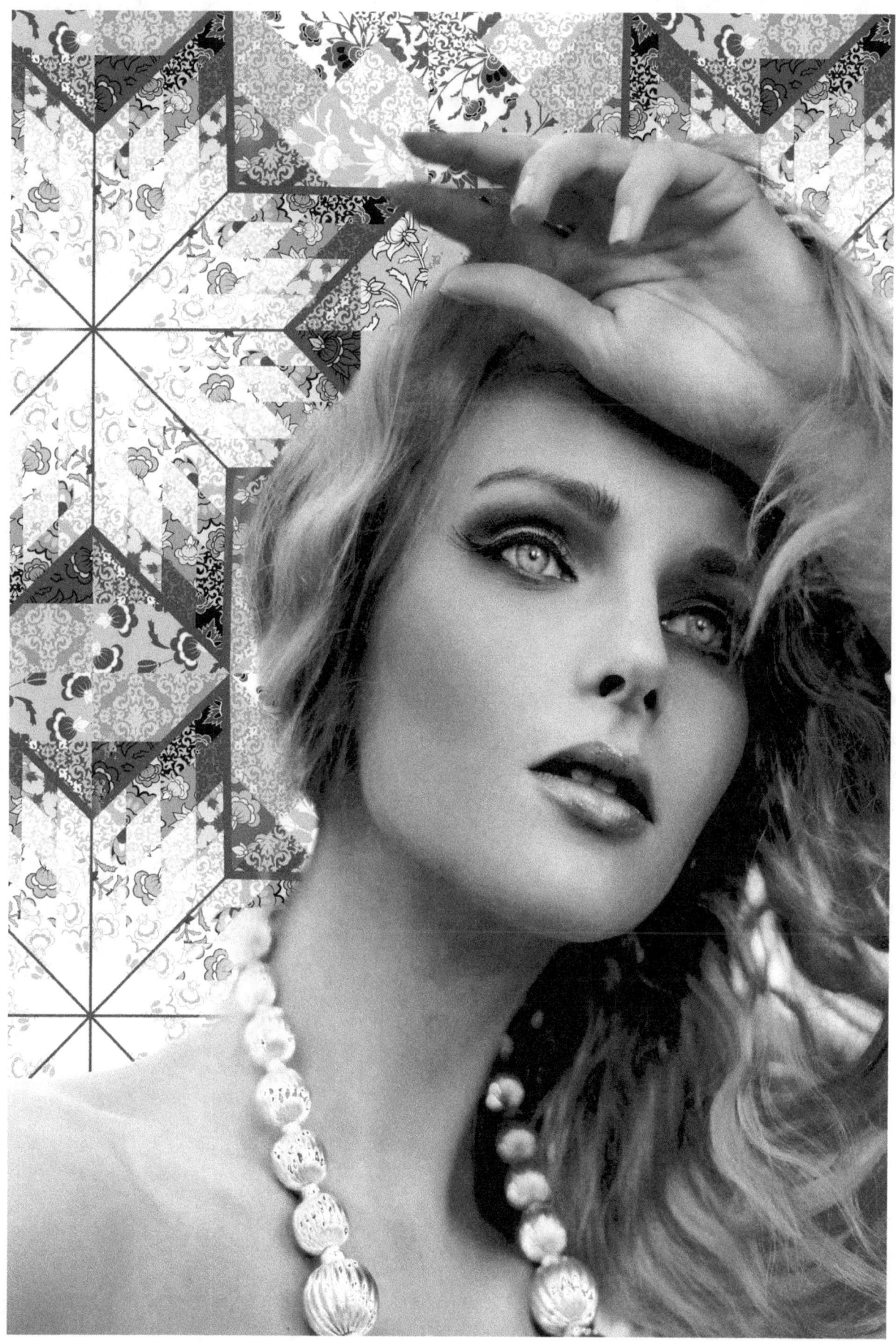

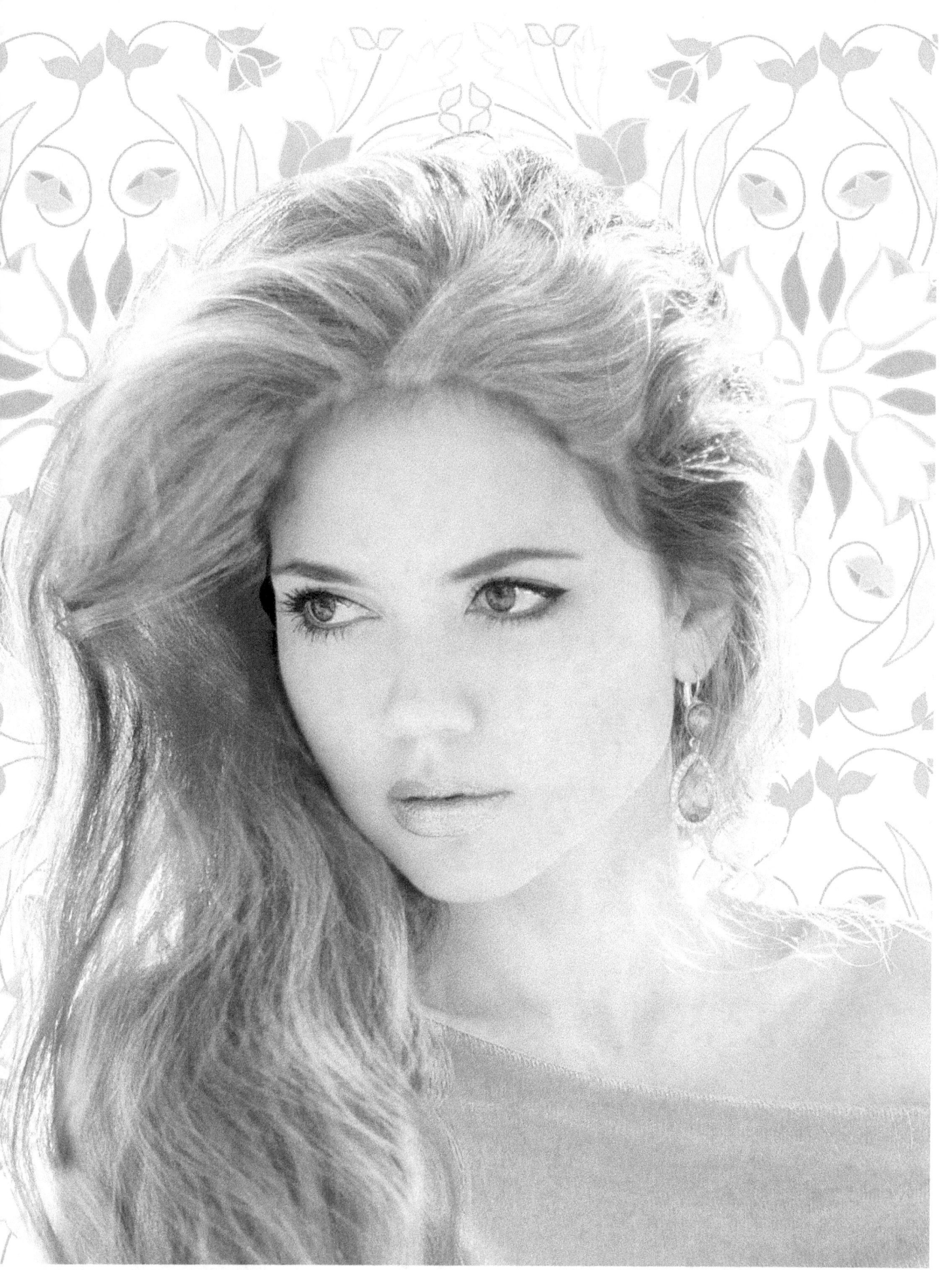

24

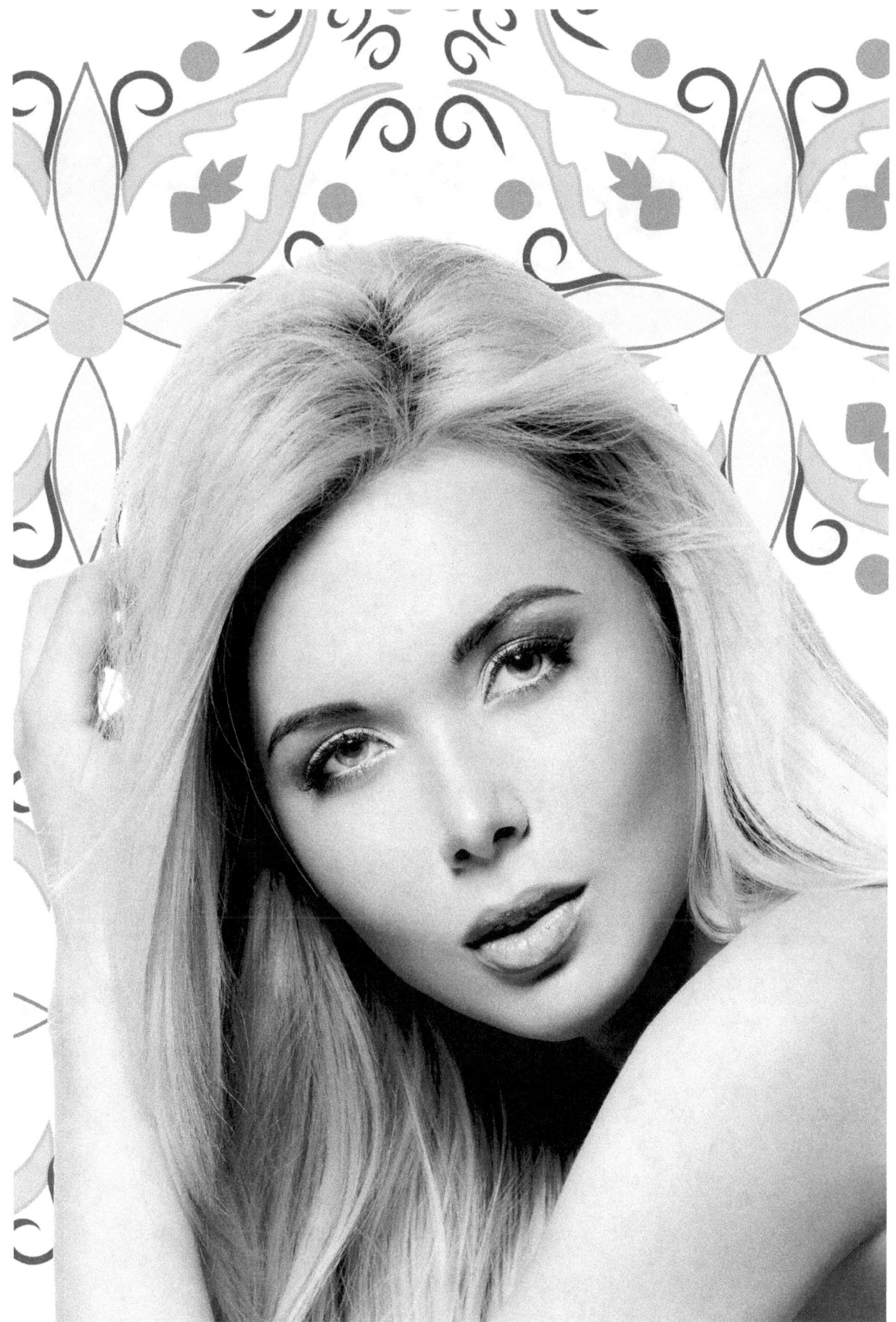

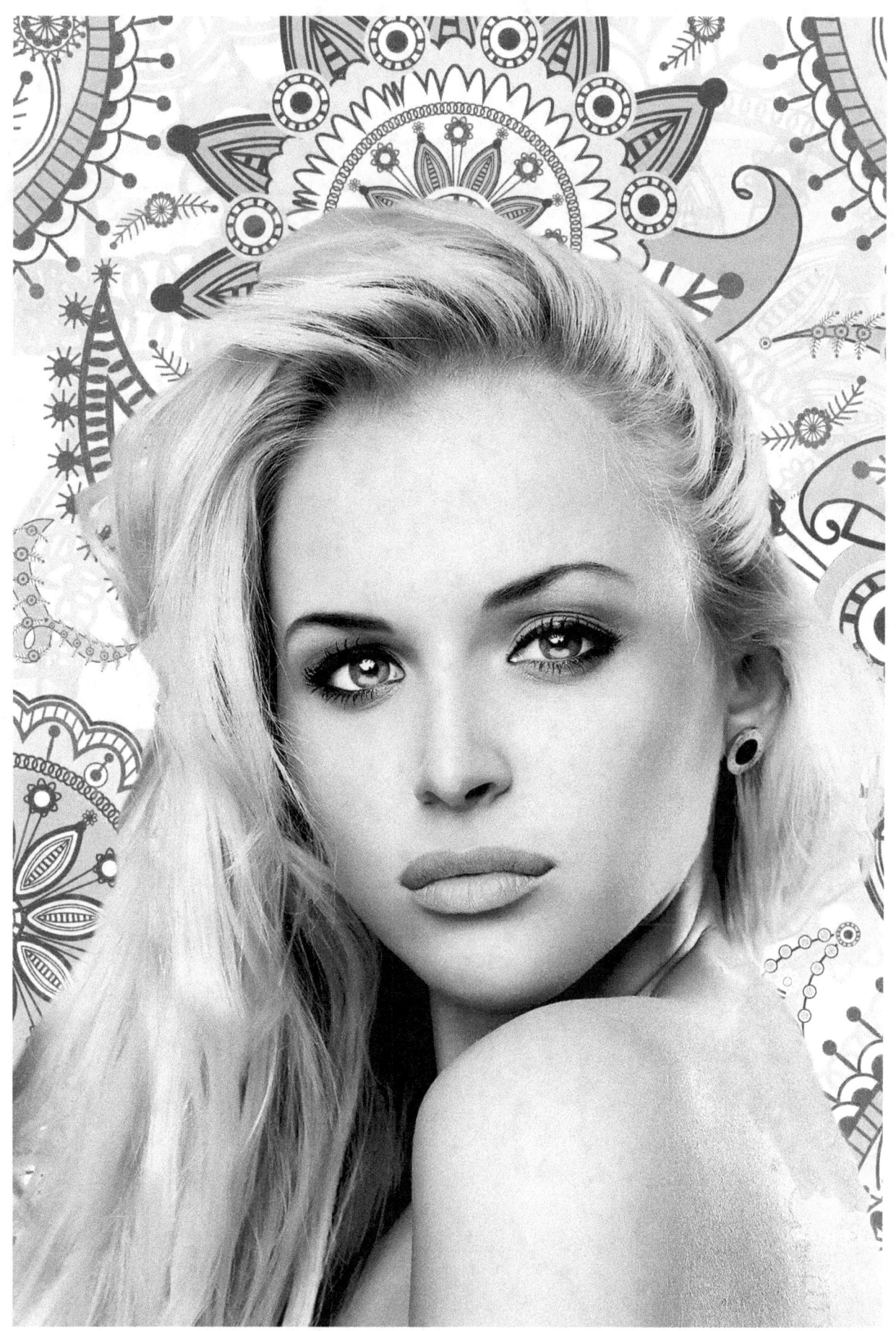

28

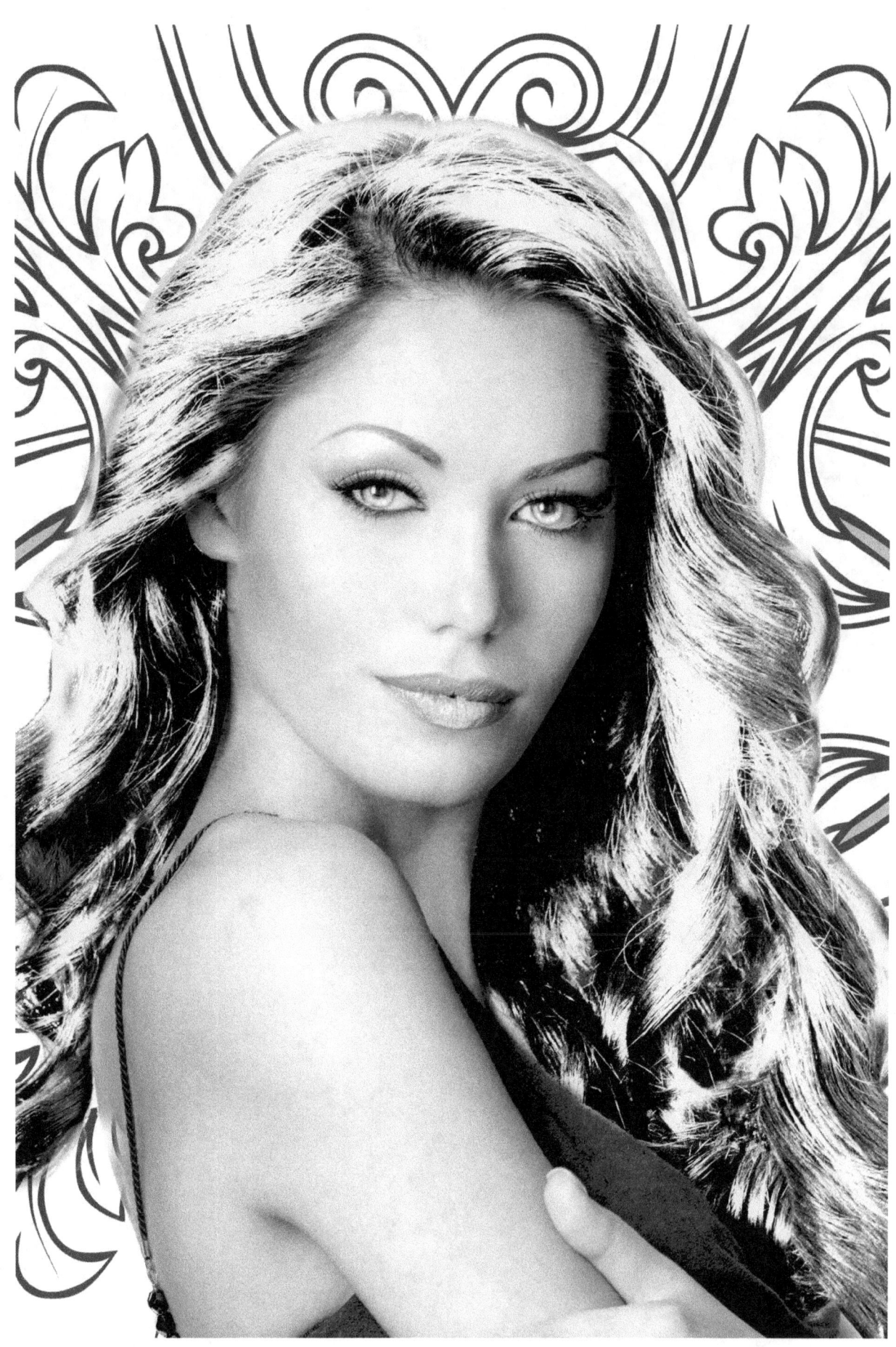

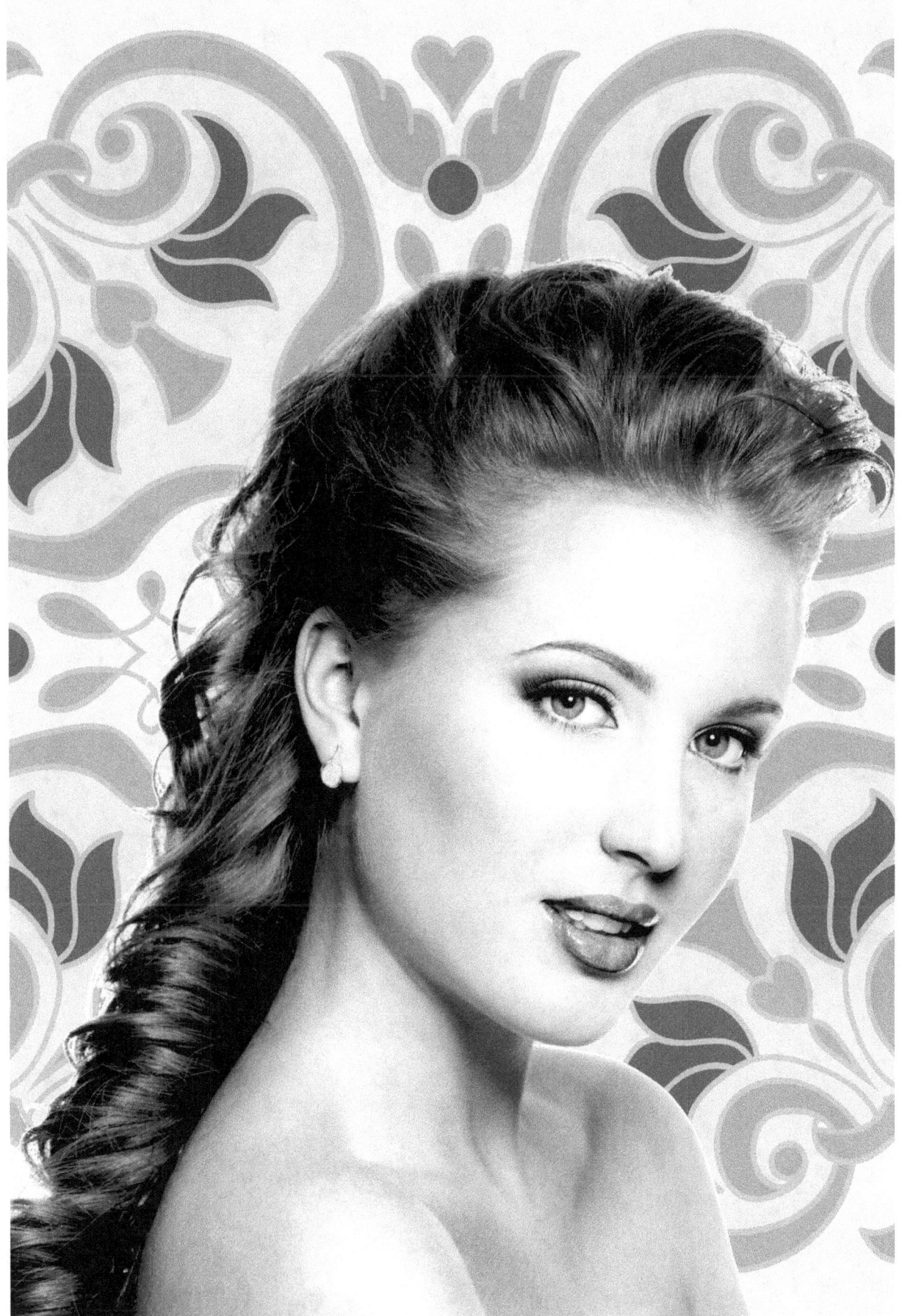

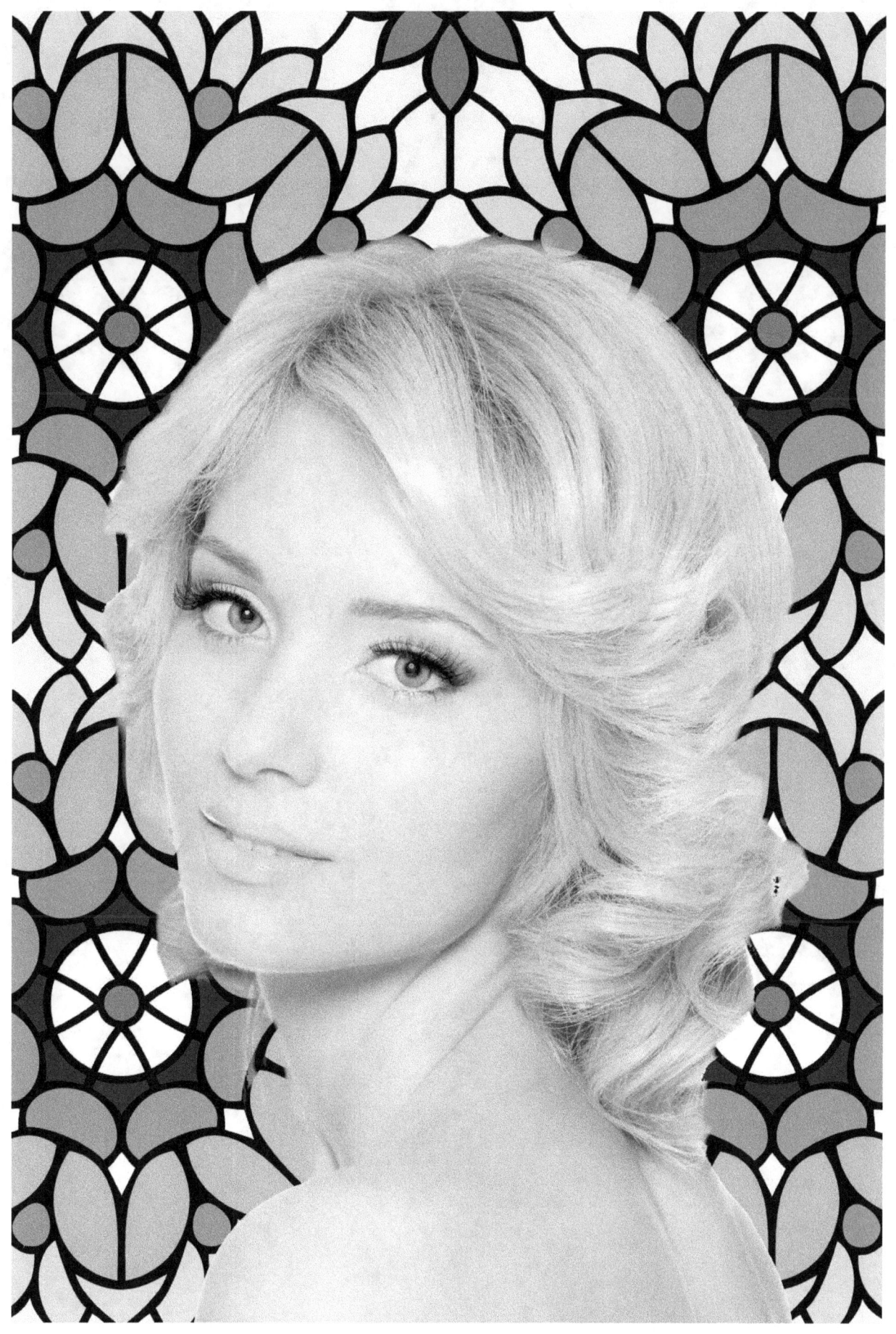

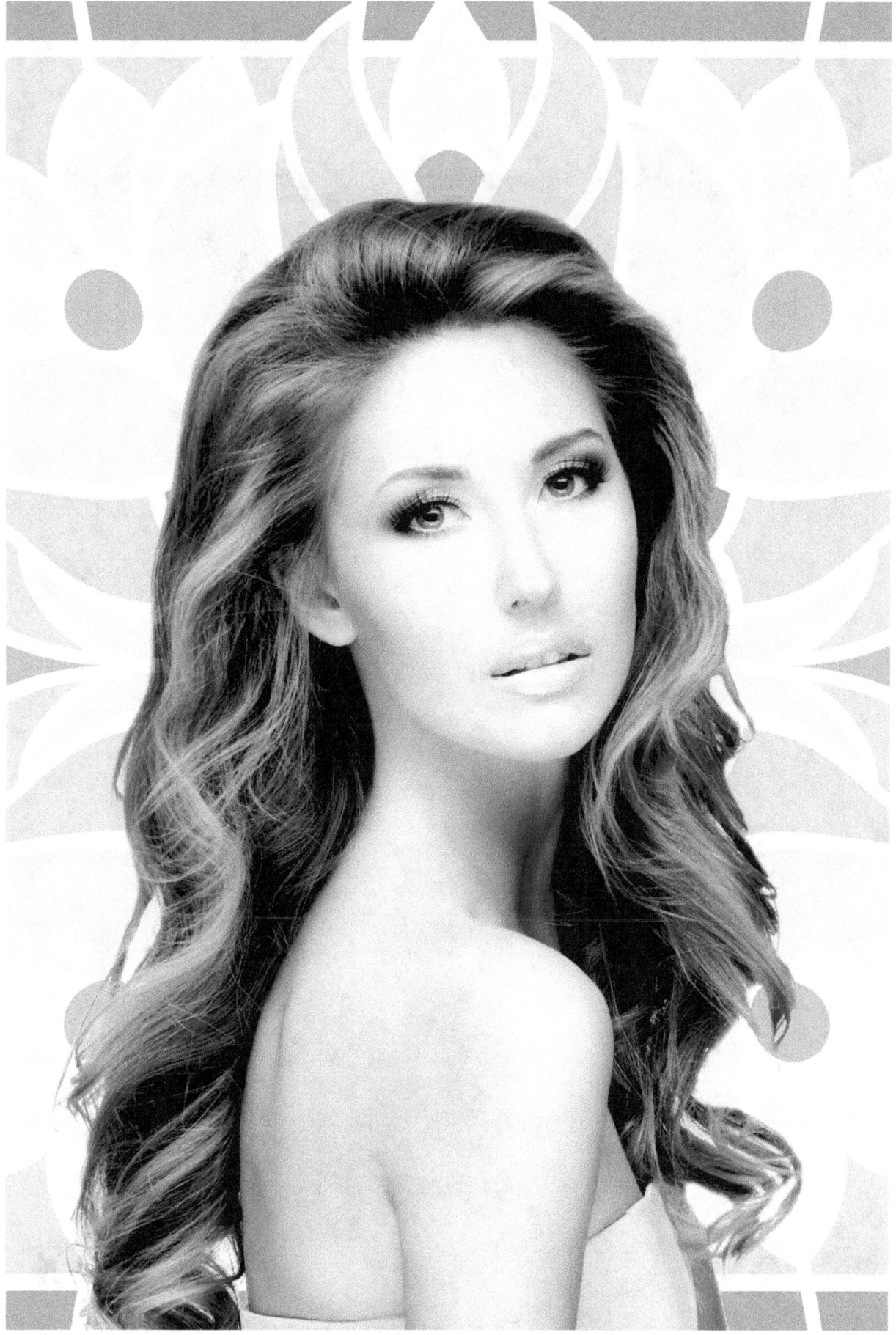

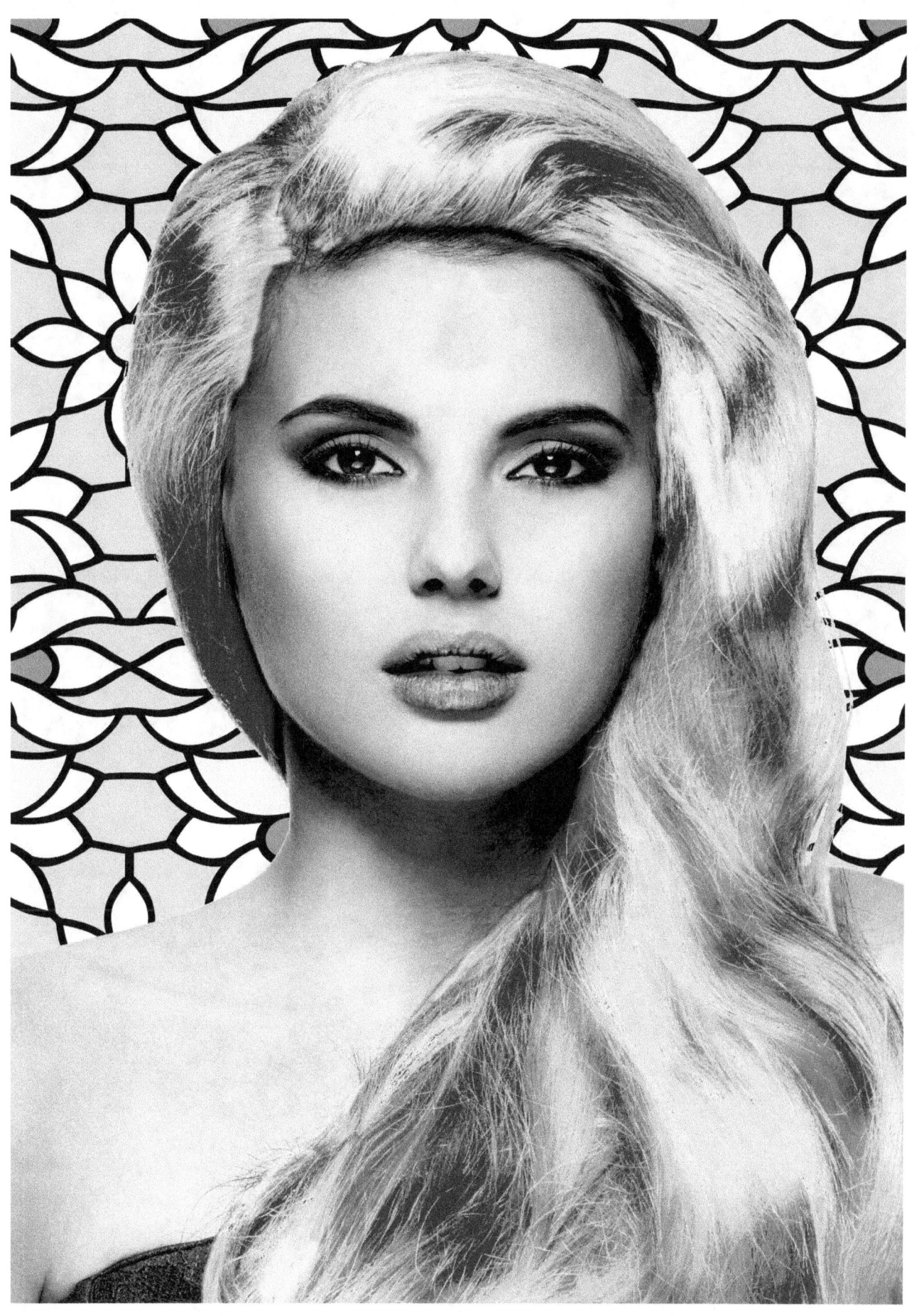

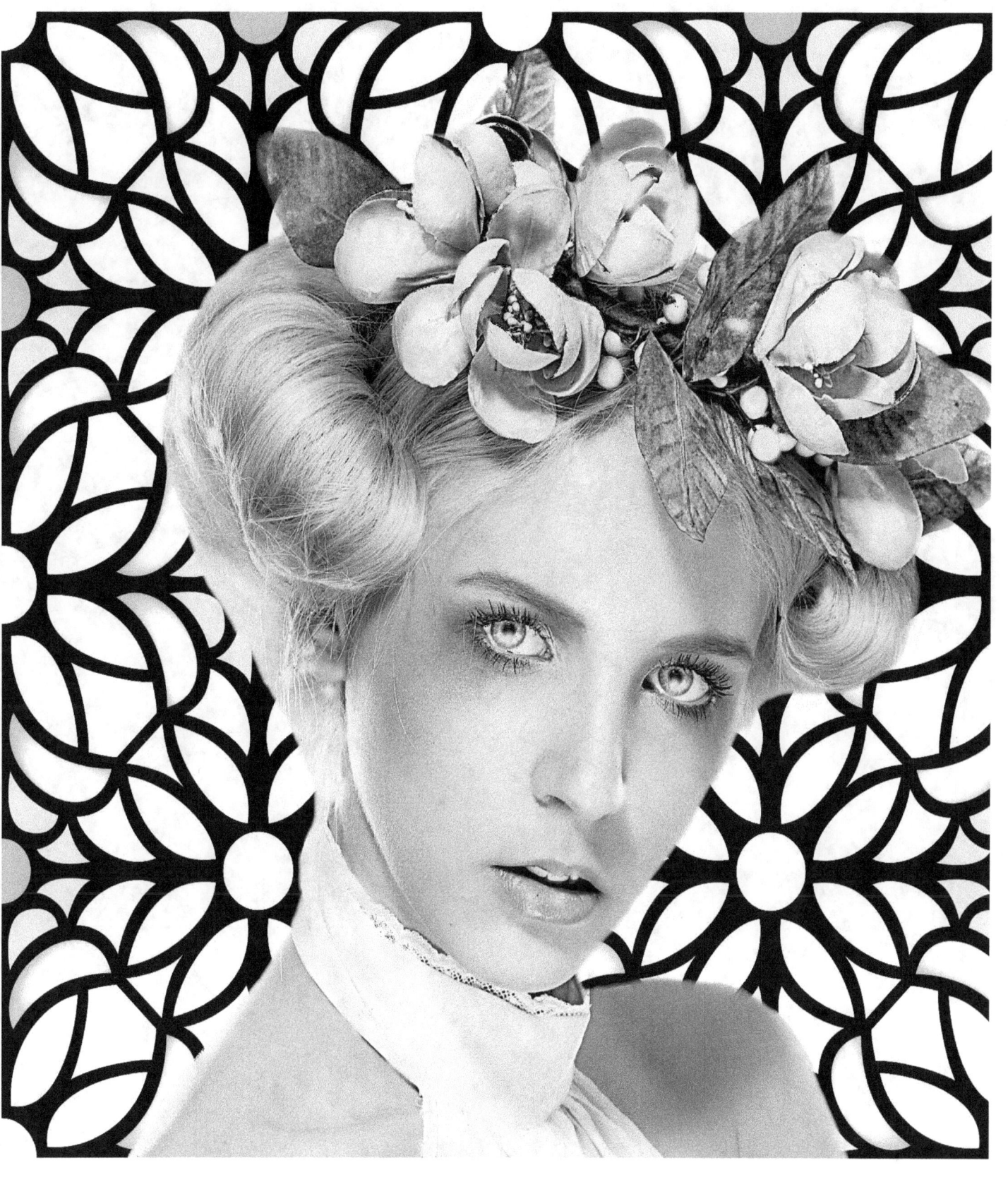

40

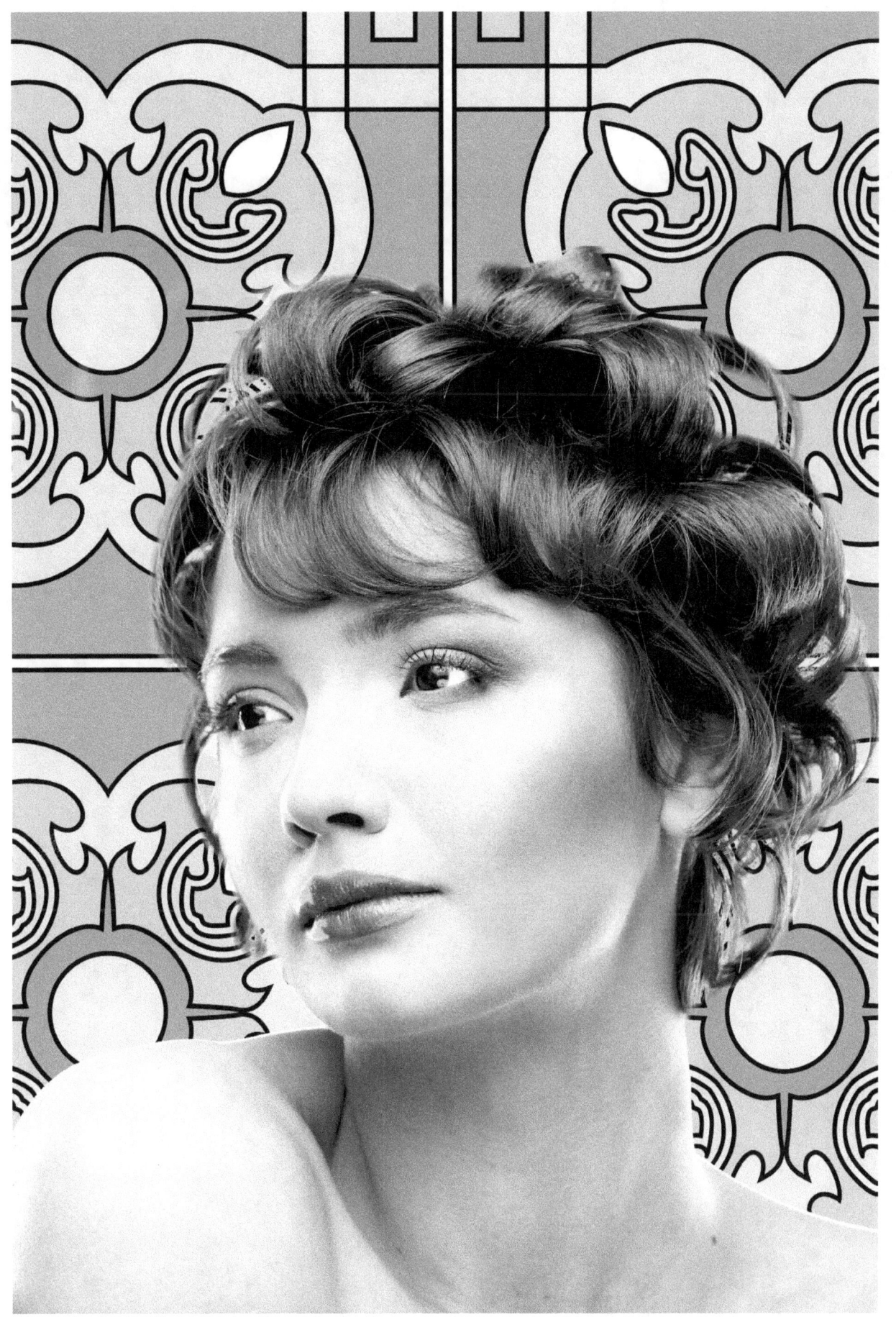

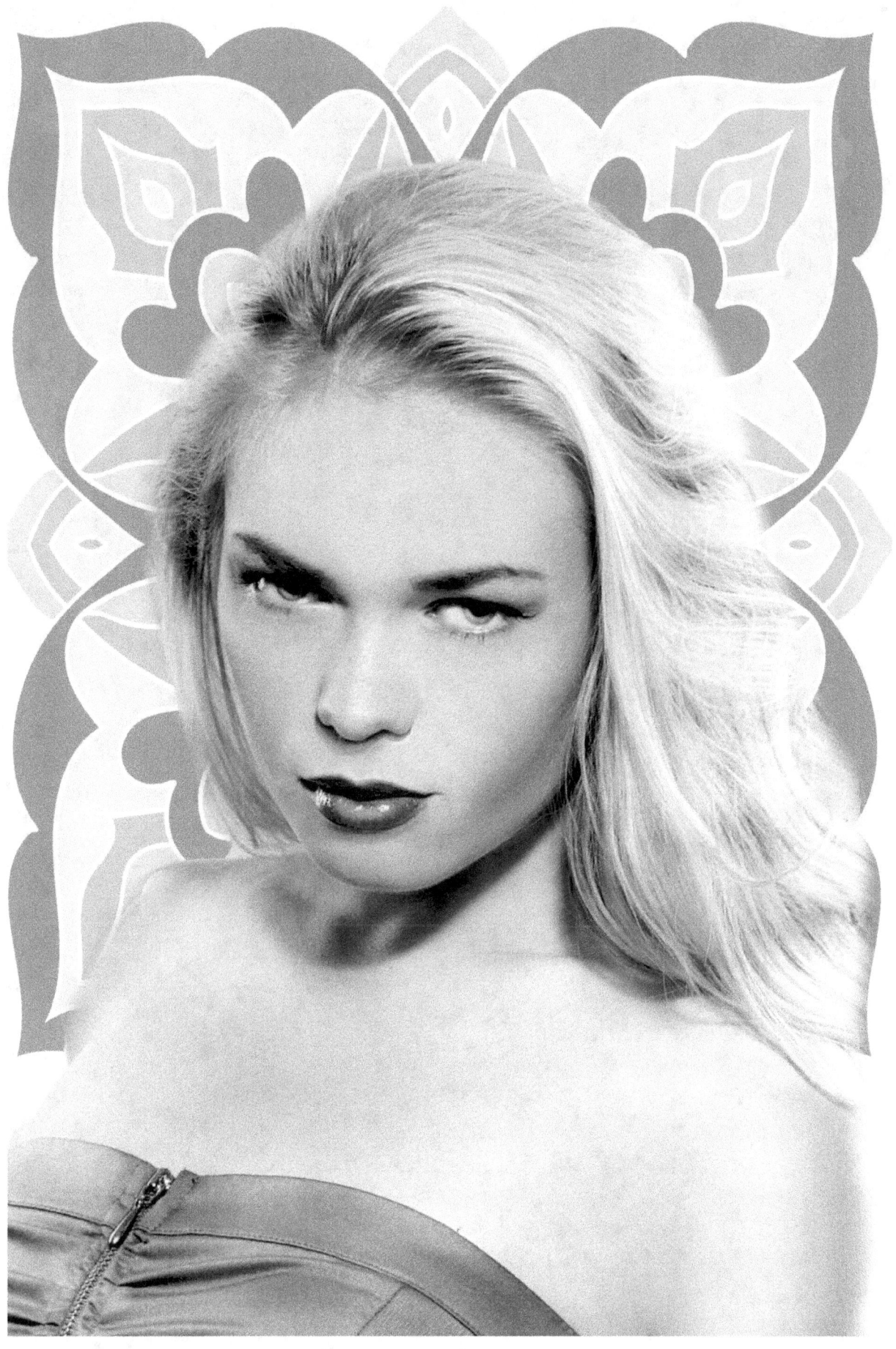

44

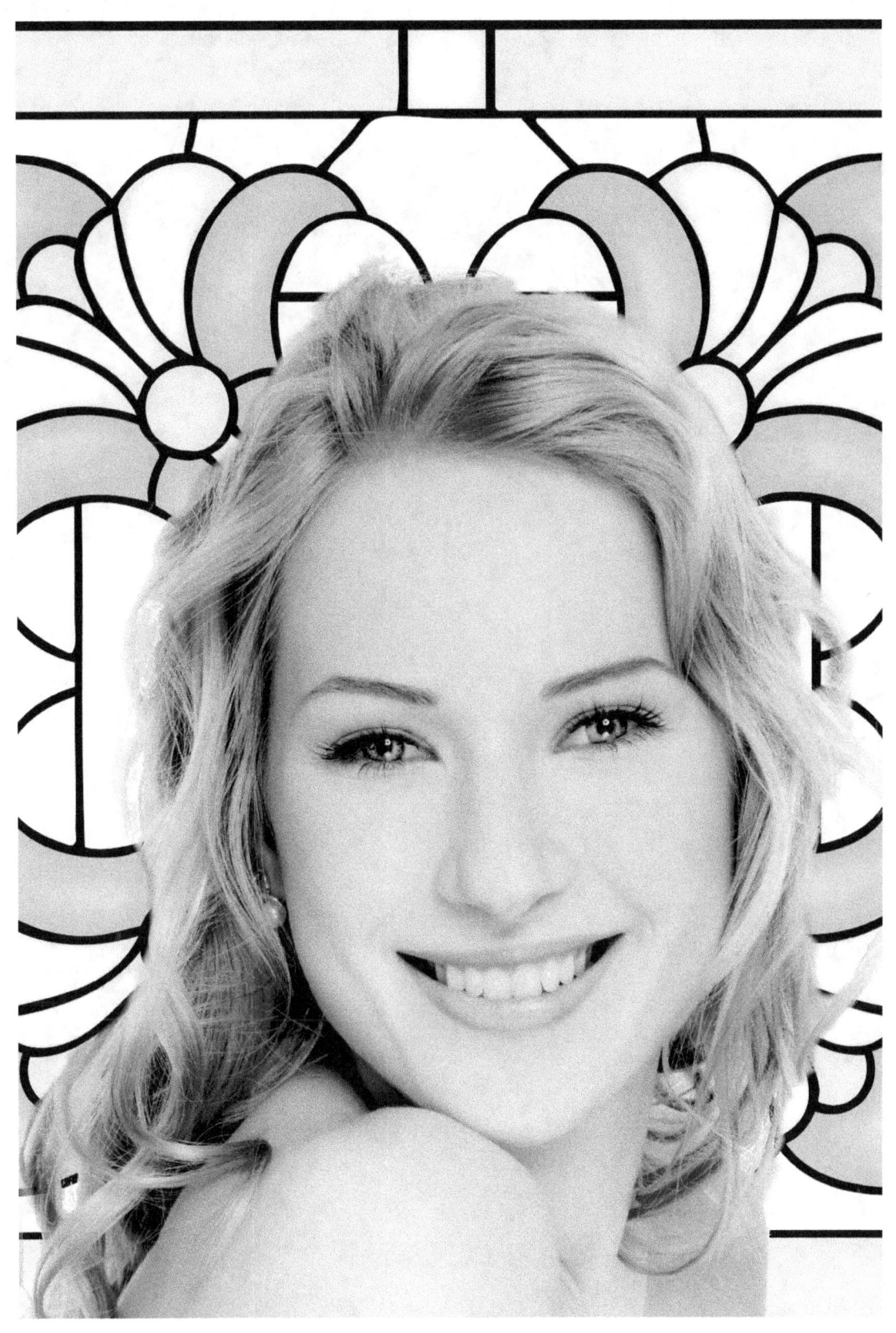

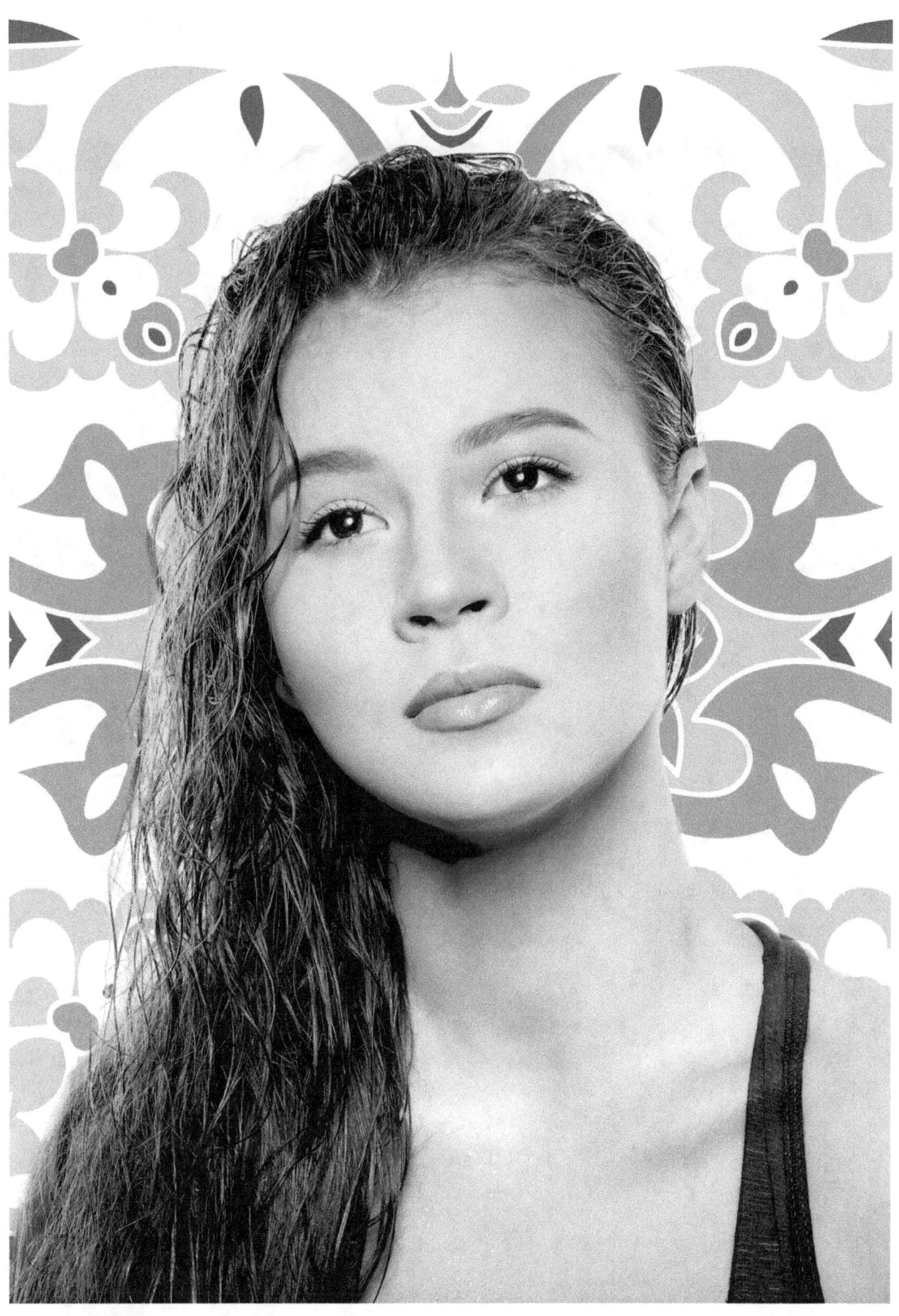

48

REVIEW REQUEST

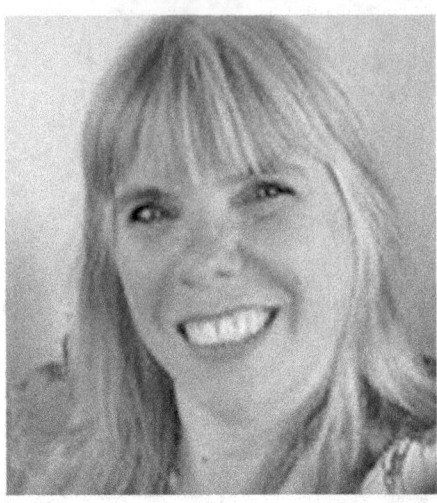

Donna was raised in rural Indiana, and after serving in
the military, she moved to rural Kentucky. She has been
creating designs for her own pleasure for nine years,
and only recently turned to publishing them.
She lives with her husband on their nine acre farm
 surrounded by woods and fields. They have a blended
 family of 7 sons and 4 grandchildren.

Coloring is a Lifestyle. What is yours?

ColoringLifestyles.com